Here's To Hope

40 Days Of Pursuing Hope In Jesus

Sterling Edwards

The characters and events portrayed in this book are fictitious. Any similarity to real persons, living or dead, is coincidental and not intended by the author.

ISBN-13: 9798854620048
ISBN-10: 1477123456

Cover design by: Art Painter
Library of Congress Control Number: 2018675309
Printed in the United States of America

To Jenna, Madison, Braden, Emma, Avery, Charlotte, Luke, and Ezra,

This book is dedicated to each of you. Your faith in Jesus and your resilience in the face of adversity have been a source of inspiration and strength for me.

May these words serve as a reminder of the unyielding hope we have in Jesus and the unwavering love we share as a family. Together, we will continue to navigate life's challenges, knowing that our hope in Jesus will never disappoint.

Here's To Hope,

INTRODUCTION

Welcome to "Here's To Hope," a 40 Day devotional book that seeks to illuminate the path of hope in the midst of life's trials and uncertainties. In these pages, we embark on a journey of faith, exploring the transformative power of hope anchored in the person of Jesus Christ.

Each day brings its own set of challenges. In times of difficulty, it is easy to become overwhelmed and discouraged, questioning the purpose and meaning behind our struggles. Yet, it is precisely in these moments that hope becomes essential.

This devotional book is born out of the belief that hope is not a fleeting emotion or a wishful thinking, but a powerful force that sustains us through the storms of life. "Here's To Hope" encourages us to place our trust in the unchanging nature of God and His promises, knowing that He is with us in every season and circumstance.

Together, we will delve into inspiring passages from the Scriptures, each revealing the depth of God's love and faithfulness. We will encounter the life-transforming grace of Jesus Christ, discovering that His sacrifice on the cross is the ultimate source of hope and restoration.

"Here's To Hope" invites you to embrace the truth that God is working all things for good, even in the midst of life's most challenging circumstances. As we turn our eyes towards Jesus, we find hope that transcends our circumstances, transcends our failures, and transcends our limitations.

May this devotional book be a source of encouragement, a reminder that hope is not elusive or distant, but a gift that is freely offered to us through Jesus. Let us journey together towards a deeper understanding of God's unwavering love, His boundless grace, and His unshakable hope.

Here's to hope, for today and every day.

HERE'S TO HOPE

DAY 1

God Is With Us. God Is For Us.

Psalm 32:5

Finally, I confessed all my sins to you and stopped trying to hide my guilt. I said to myself, "I will confess my rebellion to the Lord." And you forgave me! All my guilt is gone.

The Lord is with us at all times.
We cannot isolate ourselves from Him.
We cannot hide.
We cannot pretend He is not there.

God sees us.
God knows us.
God loves us.

But, the Enemy is crafty. He sets a trap for us to believe God is not present.

And, if God is not present, then what does it matter if we live selfishly?
What does it matter if we disregard what God says?
What does it matter if we disregard everyone else?

The Enemy convinces us that we don't really need anybody.
He convinces us that everything is fine.
He convinces us that we should just leave everything alone.
And, that is exactly what happens.

We feel alone.
We feel beyond God's grace.
W1e feel beyond the reach of God.

We feel beyond the understanding of a friend.
We feel that we have no one.

So, whether we feel that we have been isolated by others,
or,whether we have isolated ourselves,
we have learned to keep everyone, including God, at a distance.

Everyone is vulnerable to isolation.
But, isolation is always a trap.
It's always a tactic by the Enemy to keep us from coming to the only One who can actually set us free, the One who can actually forgive our sins, and the One who actually covers us with His grace.

Don't fall for it.
God is near.
God is here.
God is with us.
God is for us.

We do not have to hide for another moment.

Here's To Hope: *Let's embrace the truth that God is always with us, offering His unwavering support and grace. In times of isolation, we can turn to Him and find refuge, knowing that we are never truly alone. With hearts open to His love, we can break free from the Enemy's trap, experience the joy of God's forgiveness, and walk in the assurance of His abiding presence.*

DAY 2

Speak Up.

Ephesians 4:29

Let no corrupting talk come out of your mouths, but only such as is good for building up, as fits the occasion, that it may give grace to those who hear.

It's easy to be critical.
It's easy to become cynical.

We can question whether they are doing it right.
We can question whether they are doing it for the right reason.

There will be no shortage of opportunities to be critical today.
There will be numerous chances to be cynical today.

But, we have enough critics and cynics.
We have enough eye rollers.
We have enough skeptics.

Be a different voice.
Look for the chance to encourage.
Look for the opportunity to cut someone some slack.
Look for the situation where you can extend grace.
Look for the chance to build someone else up.

Don't underestimate the impact of your words.
Don't underestimate the difference that your response can make.
Don't underestimate what God can do.
Don't underestimate who God can use.

Here's To Hope: *So, on this day, let us seek opportunities to speak encouragement into the lives of others. Let our words be filled with grace, understanding, and love, making a difference in the lives we* *touch. As we become vessels of God's grace, we will experience the joy of being part of His transformative work in the world.*

DAY 3

Just As You Are.

Hebrews 4:16

Let us then approach God's throne of grace with confidence, so that we may receive mercy and find grace to help us in our time of need.

None of us have to perform today.
None of us have to pretend to be more than we are.

We can get off of the treadmill of life.
We can rest.

We can come before Jesus today and know that He actually loves us.

We can come before Jesus today and know He's not holding a scorecard in one hand and a pen in the other.

We can come before Jesus today and know He is not rolling His eyes thinking that He has already heard all of our excuses.

Jesus welcomes us today.
Jesus invites us to Himself today.

Jesus stands ready to rescue us, restore us, and redeem us.

Don't hesitate.

Jesus wants to meet with you today.

Here's To Hope: *As we go about our day, let's remember that we don't have to carry our burdens alone. We can approach God with confidence, knowing that His love and grace are available to us at any moment. So, take the opportunity to come before Jesus today,* *bask in His love, and experience the freedom of being accepted just as you are.*

DAY 4

He Won't Let You Go.

Joshua 1:9

Haven't I commanded you: be strong and courageous? Do not be afraid or discouraged, for the Lord your God is with you wherever you go.

As a Youth Pastor for many years, there were numerous times I took our students to a camp where we would participate in team building exercises and various aspects of the ropes course.

Nearly every time we brought a group of students, there was some rendition of a trust fall. The students would stand at the edge of the picnic table, or whatever other platform, cross their arms, and fall straight backwards into the arms of the other 6-8 people who had locked their arms together to insure the safe landing of the student who had taken the leap of faith.

After nearly all of our young middle school students had taken a turn, their focus turned to me.

"Sterling, let us catch you. We won't drop you. We promise."

I looked around at the well-meaning students. I didn't do all of the math, but I was pretty sure I outweighed most of them combined.
They continued, "we trusted you, we want you to trust us."

Ever so reluctantly, I climbed to edge of the picnic table.
I fell backwards.
They didn't catch me.
They blocked my fall.
They prevented me from a complete crash to the ground.
But, I don't think it would be accurate to say that they caught me.

Some of us know what this is like in real life.
Someone told us to trust them.
Someone told us why we should trust them.
We trusted.
But, they didn't catch us.
Somewhere, trust was broken.
In some way, trust was violated.
And that makes us hesitant to trust again.

We are more reluctant to climb up on the picnic table the next time.
We are more guarded when someone tells us to trust them.
We are more cynical.
We are more skeptical.
Cynicism and skepticism run deep for a lot of us.
We are guarded.
We hold back.

I get it.
I know what it is to be hesitant to trust.
But, here is also what I know.
Not trusting doesn't work either.

Living a life of compete cynicism and skepticism is the path to absolute loneliness.
I know that we cannot be an open book for everybody all of the time.
But, don't write the entire world off.

Sometimes the person who let us down deserves another chance.
Not every single time, but sometimes.
Sometimes we need to set boundaries.
Sometimes we need new friends.
But, learning to trust again is absolutely vital for our lives.

Jesus knows about broken trust.
Jesus was betrayed.
Jesus was denied.
Jesus was forsaken.

I'm not just talking about the disciples in the Bible.

I know what it is to make a promise to God and break it.
I know what it is to not follow through.
I know what it is to follow Jesus on my own terms.
I know that I have portrayed behavior that is less than trustworthy.
But, that is not the end of my story with Jesus.

No matter what I have done, Jesus has never turned His back on me.
Jesus has never changed His mind.
Jesus has never dropped me.

Jesus invites me and you to trust Him with all we have.

Jesus tells us that we can bring him every need, every concern, every detail of our lives, and that we can trust Him with every worry, every care, and all of our anxiety.

For those of us who are reluctant to trust, this is not always easy.
But, don't let the doubt, cynicism and skepticism rob You of Jesus has for you.
Don't let what someone else has done prevent you from experiencing the One who gives us His unfailing love and is absolutely trustworthy.

Surrender.
Fall back.
Trust Him.
Rest in Him.
Jesus will not let you go.
Jesus will not let you down.

Here's To Hope: *Let's be willing to take the risk of trusting again, knowing that Jesus is the One who can heal our hearts, restore our faith, and lead us into a deeper relationship with Him. Trusting in His love and grace, we can find the courage to embrace the hope He offers and let go of the burden of skepticism and cynicism.*

DAY 5

Be Strong. Be Courageous.

Deuteronomy 31:6

Be strong and courageous. Do not fear or be in dread of them, for it is the Lord your God who goes with you. He will not leave you or forsake you.

IT'S BE STRONG AND VERY COURAGEOUS

It's not turn around.
It's not try again when it looks easier.
It's not polling to see if everyone else agrees.
It's not making sure no one gets upset.
It's not when it's more convenient.
It's not retreat.
It's not tomorrow.

IT'S DO NOT FEAR

It's not living in intimidation.
It's not conceding this is just how it is
It's not listening to their voices rattle in your head
It's not wishing they were weaker
It's not sitting back
Its not giving up
It's not over

IT'S FOR THE LORD YOUR GOD GOES WITH YOU;

It's not going it alone.
It's not fighting in our strength.
It's battling in our own power.
It's not sheer determination.

It's not willing it to happen.
It's not deciding the odds are in our favor.
It's not I don't need anyone to help me.

IT'S HE WILL NEVER LEAVE YOU NOR FORSAKE YOU.

It's not when everything goes according to plan.
It's not when things seem smooth.
It's not when there is freedom from conflict.
It's not when everything is clear.
It's not when everything makes sense.
It's not when there is a lack of chaos .
It's not just when you feel God is near.

Here's To Hope: *Let's face our fears, conquer our doubts, and press on with courage, knowing that the Lord our God is always by our side. With God as our constant companion, we can navigate life's journey with hope, perseverance, and the assurance of His unending grace.*

DAY 6

Rest In The Rescuer.

Romans 7:24-25

What a wretched man I am! Who will rescue me from this dying body? I thank God through Jesus Christ our Lord! So then, with my mind I myself am a slave to the law of God, but with my flesh, to the law of sin.

Many of us know what it is to live as a struggler.
We want to do what is right, but we don't.
We don't want to do what is wrong, but we do.
We decide we need to try harder,
but it becomes even harder than before.
We become tired.
We become discouraged.
We begin to question our love for God and God's love for us.

Some of us have experienced this as an ongoing cycle in lives.

But, the cycle does not have to continue.
There is rest available to us.
There is a Rescuer available to us.

Jesus invites us to look at what He has done for us.
All of our attempts and failures,
All of our fits and starts,
All of our strife and struggles,
Lead Us To The Realization That We Need A Savior!

Jesus is not asking us to Save Ourselves.
Jesus is Saving Us From Ourselves.

The Rescuer Is Inviting Us To Rest In What He Has Done For Us.

Rest in the gravity of His Grace.
Rest in the depth of His Love.
Rest in thinking about the Cross.
Rest in the power of His Resurrection.

The cycle stops when we confess that we cannot do what God is asking us to do without Him providing His power.

The cycle ends when we recognize the depth of our desperateness and our need for His strength.

God's power and God's strength are available for us today.
God's grace, God's mercy, and God's love are abundant today.

Rest In The Rescuer.

Here's To Hope: *Let us embrace the rest that comes from surrendering our burdens to Jesus. We can find comfort in knowing that our weaknesses and failures do not define us, for in Christ, we are made whole and complete. With gratitude, we can turn to our Rescuer, finding hope and strength to face each day, knowing that His power and love are more than enough for us.*

DAY 7

God Is Good, Ready To Forgive, and Full Of Unfailing Love.

Psalm 86:5
O Lord, you are so good,
so ready to forgive,
so full of unfailing love
for all who ask for your help.

You can regret it.
You can replay it.
You can rehash it.
You can repeat it.
Again and Again and Again.

Or, You Can Repent,
Ask Him To Forgive,
And Trust In His Unfailing love.
He is that Good!

We are confronted with the reality of our past mistakes and regrets. We may find ourselves constantly replaying and rehashing our wrongdoings, leading to feelings of guilt and shame.

However, the message of hope reminds us of a better alternative—to repent and seek forgiveness from God. Instead of dwelling in our regrets, we are encouraged to turn to Him, asking for His mercy and grace. God is always ready to forgive, and always abounding in unfailing love for those who seek His help.

We don't have to be burdened by the weight of our past mistakes; instead, we can trust in God's willingness to forgive and extend His love and grace to us.

When we come before God with a repentant heart, seeking His forgiveness, He is quick to respond with His unfailing love.

Here's To Hope: *Let us release the chains of regret and self-condemnation. Instead, let us embrace the hope of forgiveness and love offered by our compassionate God. With humility, we can turn to Him, knowing that His grace is more than sufficient to cover our faults.*

DAY 8

He Knows How. He Knows When.

Philippians 4:19
And my God will supply all your needs according to His riches in glory in Christ Jesus.

He came through then.
He'll come through again.
He always knows how.
He always knows when.

God's ways surpass human understanding, and He knows precisely how to meet our needs, often in ways we cannot comprehend at the moment. His timing is perfect, and He orchestrates every detail of our lives.

As we navigate life's uncertainties, we find hope in the knowledge that God is not constrained by human wisdom or earthly limitations. He provides for us in ways that we may not immediately comprehend, but ultimately lead to our benefit.

Our hope is not confined to the past; it eagerly anticipates the future. God's nature remains unchanged, and His promises are unwavering. As we encounter new challenges and uncertainties, we can trust that God will come through for us once more. His abundance knows no bounds, and He is not limited by our circumstances. When we place our trust in Him, we can rest assured that He will provide for us according to His perfect plan and timing.

Here's To Hope: *In times of doubt and insecurity, we can anchor our hope in God's unchanging character and past faithfulness. He is the provider of our needs, and His love and care extend throughout eternity. As we move forward, let us trust in His unfailing provision, knowing that He has come through for us before, and He will do so again in His perfect timing and in ways beyond our comprehension. With hearts full of hope, we can confidently face life's uncertainties, secure in the knowledge that our God is always faithful and will never forsake us.*

DAY 9

The Grace Of Jesus Is Greater.

Romans 5:20

But where sin multiplied, grace multiplied even more.

Greater than our sin.
Greater than our stubbornness.
Greater than our stupidity.
Greater than our shame

We make mistakes, struggle with our weaknesses, and carry the burden of shame. Yet, in the midst of our shortcomings, there is a beacon of hope— the incredible, overwhelming grace of Jesus.

No matter how grave or numerous our sins may be, the grace of Jesus is greater. His sacrificial love on the cross paid the price for our sins, providing us with a path to reconciliation with God. His forgiveness knows no bounds, offering us a chance to be washed clean and to start anew.

Often, we resist God's calling and cling to our own ways. Yet, God pursues us relentlessly, seeking to soften our hearts and lead us back into His embrace.

We may make foolish decisions and wander off the right path, but the grace of Jesus is greater. His wisdom far surpasses our understanding, and He offers us guidance and direction, even in the midst of our folly.

Our past mistakes and failures can burden us with shame, making us feel unworthy of love and acceptance. Yet, the grace of Jesus is greater than our shame. His love covers our past and empowers us to walk in the freedom of His forgiveness.

Here's To Hope: *The grace of Jesus is indeed greater than all our shortcomings and inadequacies. It reaches into the depths of our brokenness, offering us hope, healing, and transformation. Let us embrace this magnificent grace with open hearts, for in Jesus, we find redemption and restoration beyond measure. As we experience His grace, may it overflow from our lives, touching others with the same hope and love that has rescued us. Today, let us celebrate the surpassing grace of Jesus, our Savior, and find joy in the assurance that we are deeply and unconditionally loved.*

DAY 10

Rest. Relax. Release.

Matthew 6:34

Therefore do not be anxious about tomorrow,
for tomorrow will be anxious for itself.
Sufficient for the day is its own trouble.

In a world filled with uncertainty and worries, it is easy to become anxious about the future. However, as followers of Christ, we are reminded not to be consumed by anxiety. Instead, we are called to find hope in the rest, relaxation, and release that comes from trusting in God's care for us.

Worrying about what might happen in the future only steals our peace and robs us of the joy of the present. When we constantly dwell on the uncertainties ahead, we miss out on the beauty and opportunities of today.

In the midst of life's challenges, we can find rest in God's promises and unfailing love. Instead of fretting about the future, we can surrender our worries to Him, knowing that He holds the future in His hands. Resting in God's care allows us to experience a peace that surpasses all understanding.

Rather than carrying the weight of our anxieties, we can release them to God. Releasing our worries to God frees us to walk in faith and hope, knowing that He is in control.

Here's To Hope: *Let us embrace the message of hope in God's care. Instead of being anxious about the future, let us find rest, relaxation, and release in Him. May we learn to trust in His wisdom and sovereignty, knowing that He holds our lives in His hands. As we rest in God's care, we can face each day with confidence, knowing that He will guide us through every challenge and provide for our needs. So, don't be anxious. Rest. Relax. Release. For God is with us, and His care is sufficient for each day.*

DAY 11

He Comes To Rescue us.

Luke 15:6

Then he calls his friends and neighbors together and says,
'Rejoice with me; I have found my lost sheep.'

None of us were the 99 who stayed.
All of us are that one that ran away.

We are all like the one lost sheep, broken and vulnerable, experiencing the pain of being lost and alone. Whether through mistakes, poor choices, or deliberate rebellion, we have all felt the distance between ourselves and our Shepherd.

However, the heart of hope lies in the unwavering love of our Shepherd. He never gives up on us, relentlessly pursuing the one lost sheep while still caring for the ninety-nine. When He finds us, He rejoices, and all of heaven celebrates the return of the lost one.

The parable of the lost sheep serves as a powerful reminder that no matter how far we have strayed, God's love and grace are always ready to welcome us back. His pursuit of the lost reveals His boundless love and His desire to rescue and restore us to His loving care.

Here's To Hope: *Let us find hope in the fact that we are never beyond God's reach. No matter how lost we may feel, our Shepherd is searching for us, ready to rescue us from the darkness and lead us back to the safety and love of His fold. May this assurance fill our hearts with hope and gratitude as we experience the unwavering love of our Shepherd who never gives up on us.*

DAY 12

Jesus Is Bigger. Jesus Is Better.

Ephesians 2:8-10

God saved you by his grace when you believed. And you can't take credit for this; it is a gift from God. Salvation is not a reward for the good things we have done, so none of us can boast about it. For we are God's masterpiece. He has created us anew in Christ Jesus, so we can do the good things he planned for us long ago.

As followers of Christ, we want to be people who offer real support to other people, knowing there are times when life gets really tough.

There are times when even the things that were once second nature to us, become rather difficult.

There may be moments when we feel like giving up on our goals.

There may be moments when we begin to question our purpose.

There are possibly moments when we wonder if things will change, if we are good enough, and if this all that there is.

But, there's another aspect to all of this.

Sometimes we discover, on various levels, that our best efforts are not always good enough.

We find ourselves in situations or circumstances where our will-power comes up powerless.

The habits become harder to break.
The addiction is stronger than we thought/.
The thing that we want to do, we do not do.
The thing that we do not want to do, we end up doing.

From the time that most of us are babies, we have been taught and told that we can do anything that we set out to do.

We've heard the cliches:
"The skies the limit."
"Reach for the stars."
"You've got this!"

But, nearly every single one of us face a sobering reality at some point or another in our lives.

Nearly all of us will come to a point when we realize that despite our best efforts, we are unable to save ourselves, redeem ourselves, or reconcile ourselves.

This is what is so amazing about the grace of Jesus.
The grace of Jesus is bigger than anything in our past.
The grace of Jesus is bigger than any level of hurt we have experienced.
The grace of Jesus is bigger than any pain that we have caused.
The grace of Jesus is bigger than our best efforts.
The grace of Jesus is bigger than our worst efforts.

The good news for us today is that the grace of Jesus is not waiting for us to make it from point A to point B.

The grace of Jesus is not asking us to pull ourselves up using our own strength and power.

The grace of Jesus is available to us, because that is how much Jesus loves us.

The grace of Jesus cheers us on, encourages us, and meets us even when we have nothing left to give and nothing left in the tank.

Jesus is greater than our very best efforts.
The grace of Jesus surpasses our current situations and circumstances.1

For any of us who have had a moment in our lives when we didn't really see how it was all going to turn out okay,

for any of us who couldn't see how things were going to get any better,
for any of us who couldn't see how things could possibly change,
maybe there is just one baby step to take today:

Know that Jesus cares.
Know that Jesus isn't playing hide and seek.
Know that Jesus isn't saying "catch me if you can."
Know Jesus awaits.
Know Jesus is available.
Know that Jesus is beyond any situation or circumstance.
Know Jesus is bigger.
Know Jesus is better.

Here's To Hope: *Let us embrace the amazing grace of Jesus, which is available to us unconditionally. His grace is bigger than our best efforts and surpasses any situation we may face. As we take that baby step towards Him, we can rest assured that He cares deeply for us and offers hope, love, and strength in every moment of our lives. Embracing His grace, let us find hope, knowing that we are cherished and empowered to do the good things He has planned for us.*

DAY 13

Don't underestimate what God can do.

Luke 1:37
For nothing will be impossible with God.

With God,
A + B Does Not Always = C

We often encounter situations where our limited understanding cannot comprehend the ways of God. We may face circumstances where it seems like the logical outcome would be one thing, but with God, the equation doesn't always add up as expected.

In our human reasoning, we often try to make sense of the events and challenges we face by following a logical progression. We expect that if A happens and then B follows, the natural outcome should be C. However, with God, His ways are beyond our comprehension. He is not confined by human limitations or predictable outcomes.

The Bible reassures us that nothing is beyond the scope of God's power and capability. He is the God of impossibilities, and His plans and purposes extend far beyond our understanding. When faced with seemingly insurmountable challenges, we can find hope in knowing that God's ability to intervene and work miracles is boundless.

While we may not always comprehend God's ways, we can trust in His wisdom and goodness. When we surrender our limited understanding to Him, we open ourselves to experiencing the fullness of His miraculous work in our lives.

Here's To Hope: *Let us hold on to hope in the God of impossibilities. He is not confined by our human understanding, and His plans are beyond our comprehension. As we place our trust in Him, we can find comfort in knowing that nothing is impossible with God. He is the source of our hope, and His power is at work within us, capable of accomplishing far more than we can ask or imagine. Let us walk in faith, acknowledging His sovereignty and surrendering our limited understanding to the One who holds all things in His hands.*

DAY 14

Today, there will be no circumstance beyond God's power and no situation without God's presence.

Jeremiah 32:17"*Ah, Lord God! It is you who have made the heavens and the earth by your great power and by your outstretched arm! Nothing is too hard for you.*"

Whatever circumstances we may face today, we can take comfort in the assurance that nothing is beyond God's ability to handle, and His presence is with us in every situation.

In the midst of life's challenges and trials, it's natural to feel overwhelmed or powerless. However, with God, there is no circumstance that surpasses His mighty power. He is the Creator of the universe, and nothing is too difficult for Him.

Even in the darkest moments, God's presence remains with us. His promise to never leave or forsake us provides a source of hope and comfort, knowing that we are never alone, no matter what we face.

God is not limited by time, space, or circumstance. His presence extends to every corner of our lives, guiding, comforting, and strengthening us. His all-encompassing presence is a beacon of hope, reassuring us that we can find refuge and rest in Him.

Here's To Hope: *As we face the uncertainties and challenges of today, let us hold fast to the truth that nothing is beyond God's power, and His presence is always with us. In Him, we find hope, strength, and comfort, knowing that we are not alone on this journey. His all-encompassing presence and mighty power are our source of hope and assurance. May we rest in the knowledge that with God, there is no circumstance too difficult and no situation* *without His guiding hand. Let us walk in faith, trusting in His infinite wisdom and love, and finding hope in His unfailing presence.*

DAY 15

Jesus Is Our Satisfaction. Jesus Is Our Hope.

Psalm 16:11

You make known to me the path of life;

you will fill me with joy in your presence,

with eternal pleasures at your right hand.

Jesus Will Never Provide us With Anything Or Anyone,
To Be The Source of our Satisfaction,
To Be The Source of our Hope,
Other Than Himself.

In a world filled with distractions and temporary pleasures, it's easy to seek satisfaction and hope in things or people other than Jesus.

Jesus alone is the true source of our satisfaction and hope. When we look to Him, we find lasting fulfillment that surpasses anything the world can offer.

The world may entice us with promises of instant gratification and fulfillment, but all too often, those pursuits leave us empty and unsatisfied. Jesus invites us to come to Him and find rest for our souls. In Him, we discover the true source of satisfaction that fulfills our deepest longings.

Many things in life may promise hope, but they often prove fleeting and uncertain. Jesus offers a hope that anchors our souls in the midst of life's storms. His promises are true, and His faithfulness never wavers, providing us with a hope that stands firm.

It's essential to recognize that no person, possession, or achievement can replace Jesus as the source of our satisfaction and hope. He alone can fulfill the deepest needs of our hearts. When we seek Him above all else, our lives are transformed, and our hope is secured in Him.

Here's To Hope: *Let us fix our eyes on Jesus as the true source of our satisfaction and hope. When we come to Him with open hearts, we find rest for our weary souls and an anchor that holds us steady in life's uncertainties. Jesus' love, grace, and faithfulness are unchanging, providing us with a hope that surpasses anything the world can offer. Today, may we seek Him alone and discover the abundant life and eternal hope He offers.*

DAY 16

Watch Your Words.

Proverbs 18:21
The tongue can bring death or life; those who love to talk will reap the consequences.

Words can heal.
Words can kill.
Watch what you say.
Words are real.

Words hold tremendous power. They can bring healing and life or cause harm and death.

Just as a gentle touch can soothe a wounded heart, kind and encouraging words have the power to bring healing and comfort to others. When we use our words to offer love, support, and understanding, we become agents of hope in the lives of those around us.

Conversely, harsh, hurtful, and negative words can wound deeply and leave lasting scars. The pain caused by thoughtless or malicious words can linger for a long time, affecting a person's self-esteem and outlook on life.

Our words are a reflection of our hearts. By choosing our words wisely, we demonstrate love, compassion, and empathy towards others. Being mindful of what we say allows us to build healthy and uplifting relationships.

The words we speak not only impact others but also shape our own lives. When we choose to use our words constructively and positively, we create an environment of hope and love. On the other hand, negative words can lead to isolation and the loss of meaningful connections.

Here's To Hope: *Let us recognize the incredible power of words and the impact they have on ourselves and those around us. May we use our words to bring healing, encouragement, and hope to others. By guarding our tongues and choosing to speak with kindness and wisdom, we can cultivate a culture of hope and love. Let our words be a source of inspiration and life, lifting others up and pointing them towards the hope found in Christ.*

DAY 17

Be Kind.

Ephesians 4:32

Be kind and compassionate to one another, forgiving each other, just as in Christ God forgave you.

Two Words.
Easily Forgotten.
Requires Effort.
Needs Practice.

BE KIND.

In a world filled with busyness and distractions, the simple act of kindness can be easily overlooked. Though it may require effort and practice, choosing kindness is a source of hope and encouragement to those we encounter.

These two words hold immeasurable significance. When we choose to be kind, we extend love, compassion, and empathy to those around us. Kindness can bridge gaps, mend broken hearts, and brighten someone's day.

In the midst of our daily activities and responsibilities, kindness can easily slip our minds. However, when we intentionally cultivate kindness in our hearts, it becomes a natural response in our interactions with others.

Choosing kindness may sometimes require stepping out of our comfort zones or sacrificing our time and resources. Yet, the effort invested in showing kindness is never in vain, as it has the potential to touch lives and foster a spirit of hope in both giver and receiver.

Kindness is not a one-time act but a virtue to be practiced consistently. The more we practice kindness, the more natural it becomes, and the more it shapes our character and relationships.

Here's To Hope: *Today, let us embrace the power of kindness. May we remember the impact of these two simple words - "Be Kind." As we choose kindness, let it not be easily forgotten amidst the challenges of life. Instead, let us put in the effort and practice this virtue consistently, knowing that kindness is a wellspring of hope and love. In showing kindness to others, we reflect the heart of Christ and become beacons of hope in a world that desperately needs it. May our actions and words be infused with kindness, bringing light and comfort to those around us.*

DAY 18

Absolute Rest Always Requires Absolute Trust.
Absolute Trust Always Produces Absolute Rest.

Matthew 11:28
Come to me, all you who are weary and burdened, and I will give you rest.

Absolute rest is found in absolute trust in God's faithfulness and love. As we surrender our worries and burdens to Him, we experience a profound sense of rest that transcends circumstances.

True rest goes beyond physical relaxation; it encompasses peace of mind and soul. To experience absolute rest, we must place our complete trust in God, acknowledging His sovereignty and His perfect plan for our lives.

When we trust God wholeheartedly, we release the need to control every aspect of our lives. We find peace in knowing that He holds our future and is working all things together for our good.

Trust and rest are intertwined, creating a beautiful synergy in our lives. As we trust God more deeply, we find rest for our souls, and as we rest in His loving care, our trust in Him grows stronger.

Here's To Hope: *Today, let us embrace the powerful synergy of trust and rest. Absolute rest comes when we place absolute trust in our Heavenly Father, surrendering our worries, anxieties, and burdens to Him. As we learn to trust Him more, our souls find rest in His unfailing love and faithfulness. This divine exchange of trust and rest becomes a source of hope and peace in our lives. May we continually grow in trust, finding comfort in the knowledge that God is in control, and as we rest in His loving embrace, may our trust in*

Him deepen even further. In this dance of trust and rest, we experience the fullness of hope that comes from our unshakeable confidence in our Heavenly Father.

DAY 19

Listen To The Voice Of Jesus.

John 8:10-11

Jesus stood up and said to her, "Woman, where are they? Has no one condemned you?" She said, "No one, Lord." And Jesus said, "Neither do I condemn you; go, and from now on sin no more.

That voice in your head,
The one that tears you down,
That voice that tells you how terrible you are,
The one that throws your past in your face:

That's Not The Voice Of Jesus.

The voice of Jesus:
Always invites us to repent
Always speaks of His incredible mercy,
Always proclaims undeserved grace,
And always expresses His extravagant love.

Listen To The Voice Of Jesus.

In the midst of life's challenges and struggles, it's easy to be burdened by negative thoughts and self-condemnation. We must discern between the voice that tears us down and the voice of Jesus, which offers hope, mercy, grace, and love. By listening to His voice, we can find healing and restoration for our souls.

The voice that criticizes, condemns, and reminds us of our past mistakes is not the voice of Jesus. This negative self-talk can weigh us down and rob us of hope. It's essential to recognize when this voice is speaking and counter it with the truth of Jesus' words.

Jesus' voice is one of invitation, mercy, grace, and love. He calls us to repentance, offering forgiveness and a fresh start. His words are full of hope, assuring us that we are deeply loved and cherished by Him.

Instead of condemning us, Jesus lovingly invites us to turn away from our sin and seek His forgiveness. In Him, we find the opportunity to change and grow, embracing a life of purpose and righteousness.

Jesus' mercy knows no bounds. He extends compassion and forgiveness to all who come to Him with a repentant heart. His mercy is a source of hope, assuring us that we can find restoration and healing in Him.

Jesus' grace is a gift we do not deserve. He freely offers salvation and new life to all who believe in Him. Through His grace, we find hope and the promise of eternal life.

Jesus' love for us is immeasurable and unconditional. His love casts out fear, bringing comfort, peace, and hope to our hearts.

Here's To Hope: *Let us discern the voice we listen to. When negative thoughts and self-condemnation arise, let us remember that they do not come from Jesus. Instead, let us listen to the voice of Jesus, which invites us to repent, speaks of His incredible mercy, proclaims undeserved grace, and expresses His extravagant love. In His voice, we find hope, healing, and the assurance that we are deeply loved and accepted by Him. May His words guide us on our journey, filling our hearts with hope and transforming our lives.*

DAY 20

Whenever.
Whatever.
Wherever.
Whoever.
However.

Matthew 6:10
Your kingdom come,
Your will be done,
on earth as it is in heaven.

Surrendering to God's kingdom and will is essential. No matter the circumstances or challenges we face, we can find hope and strength in yielding to God's greater plan and purpose.

Surrendering to God's kingdom and will means acknowledging that His timing is perfect. Whether we face immediate trials or long-term struggles, we can find hope in knowing that God's plans unfold in the right season.

Surrendering to God's kingdom and will involves letting go of our own desires and aligning them with His purpose. In every situation, we can find hope in knowing that God works all things together for our good.

Surrendering to God's kingdom and will means embracing His leading in every place we find ourselves. Whether in times of abundance or scarcity, we can find hope in God's provision and guidance.

Surrendering to God's kingdom and will involves recognizing His love for all people. No matter our background or circumstances, we can find hope in God's inclusive and unconditional love.

Surrendering to God's kingdom and will means trusting in His wisdom even when we cannot comprehend His ways. In times of uncertainty or difficulty, we can find hope in God's unchanging character.

Here's To Hope: *Let us surrender our hearts to God's kingdom and will. In whatever circumstance or season we find ourselves, we can find hope in knowing that God's plans are perfect, His love is steadfast, and His wisdom is beyond our understanding. As we yield to His guidance, we experience the peace and hope that come from aligning our lives with His greater purpose. May the prayer in Matthew 6:10 be a constant reminder to seek God's kingdom and will above all else, finding hope in the assurance that His ways are higher and His love is unfailing.*

DAY 21

Don't Give Up.

Don't Give In.

Don't Give Out.

Isaiah 40:31

But they who wait for the LORD shall renew their strength; they shall mount up with wings like eagles; they shall run and not be weary; they shall walk and not faint.

In moments of hardship and discouragement, remember that God's strength is made perfect in our weakness. Hold on to hope and trust that He is working behind the scenes, even when the situation seems bleak.

Temptations and trials may come, but stand firm in your faith. With God's help, you can overcome any challenge and resist the lure of sin.

When you feel exhausted and weary, remember that God's grace is sufficient for you. He will provide the strength and endurance you need to keep going.

Even when things seem hopeless, remember that God is the God of redemption and restoration. He can turn any situation around for His glory.

No matter how far you've gone or how many mistakes you've made, it's never too late to turn back to God. His arms are always open, ready to welcome you home.

God's plans for you and others are still unfolding. He is constantly at work, shaping and molding us into the people He created us to be.

God is by your side, guiding and supporting you every step of the way. You are not alone in your journey.

Just as God is working in your life, He is also at work in the lives of those around you. Have faith that He is drawing them closer to Himself.

Here's To Hope: As you face challenges and uncertainties, hold on to the hope that comes from knowing God is with you and He is not finished with you or those around you. Don't give up, don't give in, and don't give out, for God's grace and power are more than sufficient for every circumstance. Place your trust in Him, and let His unfailing love and strength carry you through.

DAY 22

Be An Agent Of Hope.

John 13:34

A new commandment I give to you, that you love one another: just as I have loved you, you also are to love one another.

Jesus,
Help Us To Look At People,
The Way You Look At People.
Help Us To Love People,
The Way You Love People.

We are called to view and love people with the same compassion and grace that Jesus demonstrated during His time on earth. By adopting Jesus' perspective, we can bring hope and healing to those around us, regardless of their background or circumstances.

Jesus looked beyond the outward appearances and saw the hearts of individuals. He recognized their struggles, pain, and potential. We should strive to see people beyond their flaws, recognizing their inherent value as God's beloved creations.

Jesus' love was unconditional and selfless. He reached out to the marginalized, forgave the broken, and offered hope to the despairing. We should seek to love others with the same love that Jesus showed us.

Jesus empathized with the struggles of those He encountered. He wept with those who mourned and extended compassion to the hurting. We should strive to be compassionate listeners and extend empathy to those in need.

Jesus offered forgiveness to those who sought it, demonstrating the power of grace and redemption. Let us be willing to forgive as Jesus forgave us, creating an environment of hope and reconciliation.

Here's To Hope: *As we seek to live with hope and purpose, let us remember to view and love people through the lens of Jesus' compassion and grace. May we be agents of hope in a world that often needs healing and acceptance. By seeing and loving people like Jesus, we can extend hope and light to those who desperately need it. Let us be vessels of God's love, offering hope to the brokenhearted and pointing others to the source of everlasting hope, Jesus Christ.*

DAY 23

Love In Action.

1 John 3:18

Let us not love in word or talk but in deed and in truth.

It's easier for people to believe that Jesus loves them, when they believe that followers of Jesus love them.

As followers of Jesus, we are called to be His ambassadors on Earth, reflecting His love and compassion to those around us. By embodying Christ's love in our actions, we can be a beacon of hope and draw people closer to Him.

Our love for others should extend beyond mere words or emotions. It should manifest in tangible acts of kindness, empathy, and compassion. When people experience Christ-like love through us, it becomes easier for them to believe in the boundless love of Jesus.

Jesus demonstrated His love for those considered outcasts and sinners. He dined with tax collectors, healed lepers, and embraced those society rejected. Let us emulate this unconditional love and reach out to those deemed unlovable or marginalized.

Listening to others is always an act of love. When we lend a listening ear to others' joys, struggles, and pain, we show that we care about their well-being. By empathizing with their experiences, we open the door for deeper connections and understanding.

Forgiveness is also a powerful expression of love and grace. When we forgive others as Christ forgave us, we model the transformative power of God's love.

Here's To Hope: *As we strive to be love in action, our lives become a living testimony of Jesus' love. When people witness followers of Christ demonstrating love, care, and understanding, it paves the way for them to see Jesus as the embodiment of love and hope. Let us embrace the responsibility of representing Christ's love on Earth and be intentional about showing love to others. By being love in action, we play a vital role in drawing people closer to Jesus and igniting hope in their hearts.*

DAY 24

Don't bother to pray for it.
It won't do any good to ask.
Don't even waste your breath.

God is never, under any circumstances,
going to provide us with anything or anyone,
that will bring us greater satisfaction than Himself.

Psalm 16:11
You make known to me the path of life; in your presence, there is fullness of joy; at your right hand are pleasures forevermore.

In our pursuit of hope and fulfillment, it is essential to recognize that nothing in this world can truly satisfy us like a deep and intimate relationship with God. The ultimate source of hope and contentment lies in knowing and experiencing God Himself.

The world offers various temptations and distractions that promise temporary satisfaction and pleasure. However, these pursuits often leave us feeling empty and searching for more. Seeking fulfillment in worldly desires can never provide lasting hope or genuine contentment.

God created us with a longing for a deeper connection with Him. When we turn our hearts toward Him, we find unparalleled satisfaction in His presence and love. True hope and contentment are found in knowing God and experiencing His abundant grace.

Seeking God's presence in prayer, worship, and meditating on His Word enables us to experience His satisfying love and peace. As we draw near to Him, He draws near to us, filling our hearts with hope and contentment.

Seeking God as our ultimate satisfaction transforms our perspective and priorities. We realize that true hope does not lie in the temporal things of this world but in the eternal promises of God.

Here's To Hope: *In the pursuit of hope and satisfaction, let us remember that God alone can fulfill the deepest longings of our hearts. As we seek Him above all else, we discover the abundant hope and contentment that comes from knowing and experiencing His love. Don't waste your energy on seeking satisfaction in temporal things; rather, focus on developing a rich and intimate relationship with God. In Him, we find lasting hope, genuine contentment, and an unwavering source of fulfillment that surpasses all earthly desires.*

DAY 25

Jesus Is Our Anchor.

Jeremiah 29:11

For I know the plans I have for you," declares the Lord, "plans to prosper you and not to harm you, plans to give you hope and a future.

If Jesus were to sit in a chair across from us this morning, He may would put down his coffee cup on the table and tell us something like this:

I am going to be with you wherever you go today.
I am going to face with you whatever you face today.
I will not leave.
You will not be alone.
I will supply the strength you need to get through this day.
I will supply the power to navigate through what unfolds today.
You will go through this day fueled by my grace, my mercy, and my love.
You don't have to get caught up in yesterday.
I have covered it by my grace.
You don't have to get concerned about tomorrow.
I have that covered as well.
You are going through this day with me at your side.
I want to be at your side.
I am not angry with you.
I am not annoyed with you.
I am not accusing you.
I like you.
I love you.
I gave my life for you.
I have plans for your life.
I have places to bring you.

I have people for you to love.
I have people for you to tell about my love for them.
There is no need to feel anxious about today.
There is no need to worry about tomorrow.
I have everything you need today.
I am absolutely all that you need today.

Here's To Hope:*Jesus is the anchor of our hope and the source of our strength. His abiding presence in our lives brings comfort and assurance, enabling us to face each day with confidence. With Jesus at our side, we need not be anxious about today or worry about tomorrow. His love, grace, and mercy are more than enough for us. As we embrace His presence, we discover that He is all we need to journey through life with hope, peace, and joy. Let us rest in the assurance of His unfailing love and live each day in the light of His grace.*

DAY 26

Worship Over Worry.

Psalm 95:1-7

Oh come, let us sing to the LORD;
let us make a joyful noise to the rock of our salvation!
Let us come into his presence with thanksgiving;
let us make a joyful noise to him with songs of praise!
For the LORD is a great God,
and a great King above all gods.
In his hand are the depths of the earth;
the heights of the mountains are his also.
The sea is his, for he made it,
and his hands formed the dry land.
Oh come, let us worship and bow down;
let us kneel before the LORD, our Maker!
For he is our God,
and we are the people of his pasture,
and the sheep of his hand.

Worry-*uncertainty about my current and future circumstances*
Worship-*certainty of Who is in control of my current and future circumstances*

Worship > Worry

Worry arises from uncertainty about our circumstances, while worship stems from the certainty of knowing who is in control of our lives. As we choose to worship the Lord, we find hope, peace, and assurance in His unfailing love and sovereignty.

It is natural to feel concerned about our current and future circumstances. Life is filled with uncertainties, and at times, worry may overwhelm us. However, we don't have to stay trapped in the cycle of worry.

In times of uncertainty, we can turn our hearts toward worshiping the Lord, who is in control of all things. As we acknowledge His greatness and sovereignty, our perspective shifts, and we find comfort in knowing that He holds our lives in His hands.

Our God is the Creator of everything in heaven and on earth. The seas, the land, and all living creatures are the work of His hands. As we worship Him, we are reminded of His power and authority over all creation.

The psalmist calls us to worship, bow down, and kneel before the Lord, our Maker. In worship, we recognize that He is our God, and we are His people. He lovingly tends to us as a shepherd cares for his sheep.

Here's To Hope: *When worry tries to consume us, let us choose worship over worry. Instead of dwelling on uncertainties, we can lift our hearts in praise and adoration to the Lord, who holds all things in His hands. As we worship Him, we find peace, hope, and the assurance that He is in control of our present and future circumstances. Let us come into His presence with thanksgiving and make a joyful noise to the rock of our salvation. In worship, we experience the certainty of God's love and sovereignty, which lifts our hearts above the troubles of this world.*

DAY 27

Finding Strength Amidst Trials

John 16:33

I have told you these things, so that in me you may have peace. In this world you will have trouble. But take heart! I have overcome the world.

Life is a journey filled with unexpected twists and turns. We set out with grand plans and dreams, only to encounter roadblocks and detours along the way. Things don't always go according to our carefully crafted script, leaving us feeling overwhelmed, hurt, and lost. The weight of our struggles can be a heavy burden to bear, and at times, it may seem like we are drowning in sorrow and pain.

Yet, in the midst of it all, we press on. We take another step, determined not to lose heart. We know that even in the darkest moments, there is a glimmer of hope shining through. It is in these moments of uncertainty and pain that we are reminded of the promise spoken by the Healer, the Rescuer, the One who works in and through our difficulties.

John 16:33 echoes in our hearts, offering us a lifeline of peace amidst the storms of life. Jesus, the One who has overcome the world, beckons us to find solace in Him. He doesn't promise a life free from trials and sorrows, but He assures us that His peace is available, even in the midst of our struggles.

When the weight of the world seems too much to bear, we seek after the One who offers rest for the weary soul. We look to the Rescuer, who extends His hand to pull us out of the depths of despair. In our moments of pain, we find comfort in knowing that we are not alone. The One who has overcome the world stands beside us, offering His unwavering love and strength.

As we navigate the ups and downs of life, we learn to focus on the One who works through our circumstances. He can bring beauty from ashes, turning our trials into testimonies of His faithfulness. In our brokenness, He reveals His power, using our weaknesses as opportunities to display His strength.

So, in the midst of the struggle, we cling to hope. We fix our gaze on the One who has conquered all. We choose to take heart, knowing that our pain is not in vain, and our sorrows are not the end of the story. Our Rescuer is with us every step of the way, leading us through the darkest valleys and into the fullness of His light.

Here's To Hope: *No matter what you are facing today, know that you are not alone. The Healer walks beside you, and His peace is available to soothe your weary soul. Take heart, for the One who has overcome the world is with you, and He will carry you through every trial and sorrow. Keep pressing on, for in Him, there is hope, strength, and victory.*

DAY 28

Press On Toward The Goal.

Philippians 3:14

I press on toward the goal to win the prize for which God has called me heavenward in Christ Jesus.

Life can be filled with challenges and obstacles that tempt us to give up, give in, or give out. It's easy to feel overwhelmed and discouraged when things don't go as planned or when the road ahead seems uncertain. However, as followers of Christ, we are called to a different attitude and approach.

In Philippians 3:14, the apostle Paul encourages us to press on toward the goal for the prize of the upward call of God in Christ Jesus. This verse reminds us that we have a higher purpose and a greater calling in our lives. It's not about simply surviving or coasting through life; it's about striving towards a meaningful and fulfilling purpose that is rooted in our relationship with God.

When faced with challenges and setbacks, it's essential to hold on to hope and keep moving forward. Giving up is not an option because we have a God who is always with us and empowers us to overcome obstacles.

Temptations and distractions can lure us away from God's path for our lives. We must resist the allure of worldly pursuits and stay true to our faith and values.

The journey of faith can be tiring at times, but we are encouraged to persevere and rely on God's strength. He promises to renew our strength like eagles and lead us on the path of righteousness.

Being present and engaged in our daily lives is essential. Showing up means being fully present in our relationships, responsibilities, and opportunities to serve others.

We are called to be active participants in building God's kingdom on earth. Pitching in means using our gifts and talents to make a positive impact on the world around us.

Compassion and service are central to the Christian life. Helping others in their times of need reflects the love of Christ and demonstrates His teachings in action.

Here's To Hope: *As we press on toward the goal, we can trust that God is leading us and guiding us every step of the way. His plans for us are good, and He equips us with everything we need to fulfill His purpose. Let us embrace the challenges with faith and determination, knowing that the prize of the upward call of God in Christ Jesus awaits those who press on.*

DAY 29

Live Like Jesus. Love Like Jesus.

Philippians 2:3
Do nothing out of selfish ambition or conceit, but in humility consider others as more important than yourselves.

We may consider them annoying.
We may consider them as the source of our problems.
We may consider them as obstacles to our happiness.

People can be hard.
People can be difficult.
People are definitely going to be people.

But, the call is to consider them better.
That requires humility.
That requires patience.
That requires love.
That requires us to live like Jesus.

In our journey of faith, we often encounter challenging and difficult people. They might test our patience, frustrate us, or even be the source of our problems. It's natural to feel annoyed or bothered by their behavior. However, as followers of Jesus, we are called to respond differently.

Philippians 2:3 reminds us to approach these situations with humility and love. Instead of allowing our selfish ambition or pride to dictate our actions, we are encouraged to consider others as more important than ourselves. This doesn't mean we ignore our needs or compromise our boundaries, but it does mean we treat others with respect, empathy, and kindness.

Living like Jesus requires us to go beyond our natural inclinations and respond with compassion. Jesus himself displayed incredible humility and love during His time on Earth, even to those who opposed Him. He showed us that everyone, no matter how difficult, is deserving of God's love and grace.

Here's To Hope: *As we encounter challenging people, let us remember the call to consider them better with a heart of humility and patience. Let us strive to extend the same love and grace that Jesus extends to us, recognizing that we too have our imperfections and shortcomings. In doing so, we can create a culture of love and understanding, reflecting the character of Christ in our interactions with others.*

DAY 30

Be Still.

Psalm 46:10
Be still, and know that I am God.

Be Still.
It's not all up to you.
It's not all on your shoulders.
It's not all in your control.

We can often find ourselves caught up in the busyness and responsibilities that come our way. We carry the weight of various tasks, worries, and uncertainties, and it can feel overwhelming at times. However, in the midst of it all, there is a gentle and reassuring voice calling us to "Be still."

Psalm 46:10 offers a powerful reminder that we don't have to bear the weight of the world on our shoulders. It is an invitation to find rest and peace in God's presence.

When we pause, when we still our hearts and minds, we open ourselves up to a profound truth: God is in control.

The verse encourages us to let go of our need for control and to trust in the sovereignty of God. It's a reminder that the outcomes, the challenges, and the uncertainties are not solely up to us. We can find comfort in knowing that God is at work in our lives and in the world, even in the midst of chaos and uncertainty.

"Be still" doesn't mean we become passive or complacent. Instead, it's an opportunity to release our burdens and worries to the One who holds all things together. It's an act of surrender, acknowledging that we are not in control but that we serve a God who is.

In the stillness, we can hear God's voice, leading and guiding us. We can find peace in the assurance that He is with us in every circumstance, providing wisdom, strength, and comfort. It is in the quiet moments that we can know God more intimately and experience His love and grace in profound ways.

Here's To Hope: *In the midst of the busyness and challenges of life, let us heed the call to "Be still" and find rest in the knowledge that God is God. He is in control, and His plans for us are good. May we trust in Him and find peace in His presence.*

DAY 31

Go Deeper. Then Deeper.

Romans 11:33-36

Oh, the depth of the riches and wisdom and knowledge of God! How unsearchable are his judgments and how inscrutable his ways!
"For who has known the mind of the Lord,
or who has been his counselor?"
"Or who has given a gift to him
that he might be repaid?"
For from him and through him and to him are all things. To him be glory forever. Amen.

If we better understood just how much Jesus loves us, we would trust Jesus more.

If we could better grasp the extent of the grace of Jesus, we would worship Jesus more.

If we had a stronger belief in the depth of God's power, we would doubt less and hope more.

If we could recognize the extent of God's wisdom, we would obey God more.
Don't settle for a surface level relationship with God.
We don't know what we don't know.
Go deeper.
Then deeper.

We often find ourselves standing at the surface of God's love, grace, power, and wisdom. We experience a taste of His goodness, but there is so much more to discover, to embrace, and to be transformed by.

If we could fully understand the extent of His grace, we would be moved to worship Him with all our hearts. If we had a stronger belief in His power and wisdom, our doubts would diminish, and hope would flourish.

The passage from Romans 11:33-36 beautifully captures the awe and wonder of God's richness, wisdom, and knowledge. His judgments are beyond our understanding, and His ways are inscrutable. No one can claim to fully comprehend the mind of the Lord, and we cannot repay Him for the immeasurable gifts He bestows upon us. God's greatness is far beyond our grasp, and yet, He invites us to go deeper, to seek Him with all our hearts, and to surrender to His ways.

The call is to go beyond the surface-level relationship with God, to seek Him with a hunger and thirst for more of Him. Just as a diver explores the depths of the ocean to discover its treasures, we are encouraged to dive deep into the riches of God's love, grace, and wisdom. As we do so, we will be filled with awe and wonder at the vastness of who God is and the limitless depths of His being.
God's love is not merely a concept; it is an ocean without shores. His grace is not a limited resource; it is a fountain that never runs dry. His wisdom is not confined to human understanding; it is a boundless wellspring of insight and understanding. We are called to immerse ourselves in these unsearchable depths and to experience the transformation that comes from encountering the fullness of God.

Here's To Hope: *Let us not settle for a surface-level relationship with God. Instead, let us journey deeper, seeking to know Him more intimately, trust Him more wholeheartedly, and obey Him more faithfully. In going deeper, we will find that our doubts are replaced with hope, our hearts overflow with worship, and our lives are forever changed by the greatness of our God. To Him be glory forever. Amen.*

DAY 32

Jesus Is Enough.

Romans 8:31-32

What, then, shall we say in response to these things? If God is for us, who can be against us? He who did not spare his own Son, but gave him up for us all—how will he not also, along with him, graciously give us all things?

Today, we can rest in the Truth that our greatest achievement will not contribute one thing toward us earning the grace of Jesus.

Today, we can rest in the Truth that our very worst failure today will not separate us from the grace of Jesus.

We can rest in the Truth that the grace of Jesus is available for us today.

Jesus is for us and not against us today.
Jesus is enough for all that we need today.

As we begin our day, it's a moment to pause and reflect on the truth that our achievements or failures today will not earn or diminish the grace of Jesus in our lives. We may experience success or encounter setbacks, but neither defines our standing with God. His grace remains constant, unwavering, and freely available to us.

We can rest in the reassurance that the grace of Jesus is a gift, given out of His boundless love and not based on our performance. We don't need to strive or prove ourselves worthy; instead, we can rest in His loving embrace.

Similarly, our worst failures today will not place us out of the reach of His grace. God's grace is not conditional on our perfection; rather, it is poured out on us even in our weaknesses and struggles. Our imperfections do not disqualify us from receiving His grace, for His love is greater than any mistake we make.

We can find solace in the truth that Jesus is for us and not against us. He is our advocate, our intercessor, and our defender. He stands with us in every situation, offering His grace as a constant source of hope and renewal.

No matter what challenges we face today or what uncertainties lie ahead, we can find peace in knowing that Jesus is enough for all our needs tonight. His glorious riches are available to us through His sacrifice on the cross, providing us with all that we require—spiritually, emotionally, and physically.

Here's To Hope: *Let us rest in the boundless grace of Jesus. Let us embrace the truth that His love is not based on our performance, and His grace is more than sufficient for us. We can find comfort and hope in His promise that He will supply all our needs from His glorious riches. So, let us lay down our burdens, take a deep breath, and rest in the loving arms of our Savior.*

DAY 33

Have Faith That God Is Faithful.

Hebrews 11:1
Now faith is confidence in what we hope for and assurance about what we do not see.

Our plans may have been interrupted.
The situation isn't what we scripted.
This isn't the way we thought it would go.
It's hard to see how it gets better.
Still, we can trust God even if can't see the outcome.
We can believe God even when we don't know how it will work out.
We can have assurance that God is with us.
We can have confidence that God is not finished.
God was faithful yesterday.
God remains faithful today.
God will be faithful tomorrow.
Have faith that God is faithful.

In the midst of uncertainty and unforeseen circumstances, it's natural to feel disheartened when our plans are interrupted, and life takes an unexpected turn. We might find ourselves grappling with disappointment and confusion, wondering how things will ever improve. However, in these moments of uncertainty, we can place our trust in God, even when we cannot see the outcome.

Though the situation may not align with our carefully scripted plans, we can still choose to trust God's divine plan and His unfailing love. We may not fully understand how everything will work out, but we can hold onto the assurance that God is by our side, guiding us through every step of the journey.

Today, we can have unwavering faith in God's faithfulness. As we look back on our lives, we can see the evidence of God's faithfulness in every situation, whether in times of triumph or trials. He has proven Himself faithful in the past, and this truth remains unchanging today and into the future.

In the face of uncertainty, we can find confidence in God's promises, knowing that He is always working for our good, even if we can't see the full picture yet. Our faith is not solely based on what we can see; rather, it is rooted in hope and trust in a God who is greater than any circumstance we may encounter.

Here's To Hope: *Let us anchor our faith in God's faithfulness. Let us hold fast to the assurance that He is with us, guiding us through every step of the way. His plans for us may be different from what we expected, but we can rest in the knowledge that His plans are always perfect. Let us have faith in the unseen, for true faith is the confidence in what we hope for and the assurance about what we do not yet see.*

DAY 34

Rest. Relax. Release.

Matthew 6:34
Therefore do not be anxious about tomorrow,
for tomorrow will be anxious for itself.
Sufficient for the day is its own trouble.

In a world filled with constant demands and uncertainties, it's easy to become overwhelmed and anxious about what the future holds. The pressures of tomorrow can weigh heavily on our hearts and minds, leaving us restless and uneasy. However, Jesus encourages us not to be anxious about tomorrow.

Instead of carrying the burden of worry, Jesus calls us to find rest, relaxation, and release. He invites us to trust in God's loving provision and to focus on the present moment. Each day comes with its own challenges and responsibilities, and as we navigate them with faith and surrender, we can experience the peace that surpasses all understanding.

Rather than allowing ourselves to be consumed by thoughts of the future, Jesus invites us to live one day at a time, finding solace in His presence and provision. He assures us that God's grace is sufficient for each day's needs, and as we place our trust in Him, we can find freedom from the weight of anxiety.

We can embrace a mindset that allows us to fully immerse ourselves in the present moment, acknowledging the blessings and challenges it brings. By doing so, we learn to rely on God's wisdom and guidance, knowing that He holds our tomorrows in His hands.

Here's To Hope: *As we release our anxieties and worries to God, we open ourselves to His peace and rest. In the midst of life's* *uncertainties, we can find refuge in His promises, knowing that He is in control and has a purpose for every situation we encounter. So let us not be anxious about tomorrow but embrace each day with faith and trust, knowing that God's grace is sufficient for every step of the journey.*

DAY 35

Don't Look Backwards.

Colossians 1:13-14
For he has rescued us from the dominion of darkness and brought us into the kingdom of the Son he loves, in whom we have redemption, the forgiveness of sins.

It would not be hard to let the guilt, shame, and regret of yesterday, join us today.

We can easily focus and dwell on all of what could have done, should have done, and would have done differently.

Yet, for today, God presents us with new mercy.

We are offered undeserved grace.
We are given unconditional love.
We are not entering into this day pretending that we have no reason for our guilt, shame, and regret.

We are entering into this day aware of the price that has been paid by Jesus.

We are entering into this day knowing that Jesus has taken our guilt, shame, and regret upon Himself.

We are entering into this day aware that our sins are no longer counted against us, because of what Jesus has done for us.

Yesterday is gone.
Yesterday is over.
Yesterday is finished.

Today is a new day to embrace the mercy, grace, and love Jesus has extended to us.

We have a choice to make. We can carry the weight of yesterday's mistakes and failures, allowing guilt, shame, and regret to shadow our present and dampen our hope. Or, we can embrace the fresh start that God offers us each day, the new mercy, undeserved grace, and unconditional love that He freely extends to us.

It's natural to reflect on the past, to think about what could have been done differently or what should have been avoided. But dwelling on these thoughts can keep us trapped in a cycle of self-condemnation, preventing us from fully embracing the freedom and forgiveness that Jesus offers.

We don't need to pretend that we have no reason for guilt, shame, or regret. Instead, we are invited to acknowledge our shortcomings, knowing that Jesus has already borne the weight of our sins on the cross. He took our guilt, shame, and regret upon Himself, offering us redemption and the forgiveness of sins.

Here's To Hope: *Let us not be burdened by the past but embrace the freedom and hope that Jesus provides. Let us leave behind the weight of yesterday and walk in the light of His love and mercy. With hearts filled with gratitude, let us step into this day, knowing that we are forgiven, redeemed, and loved beyond measure.*

DAY 36

The Perils Of Pride.

Proverbs 16:18
Pride goes before destruction, and haughtiness before a fall.

Pride will always cause us to underestimate the Enemy, overestimate ourselves, and completely discount the depth of God's love.

Pride is a deceptive force that can lead us down a dangerous path. It blinds us to the true nature of the enemy, inflates our sense of self-importance, and hinders us from fully grasping the depth of God's love for us.

Proverbs 16:18 warns us about the destructive power of pride. When we are filled with pride, we become vulnerable to making unwise decisions and overestimating our abilities. It puffs us up with a false sense of invincibility, leading us to believe that we can handle any situation on our own. However, the reality is that pride sets us up for a fall, as it disconnects us from the truth and reality of our dependence on God.

In the face of pride, humility becomes our safeguard. Humility allows us to acknowledge our limitations and weaknesses, recognizing that we are not self-sufficient beings. When we embrace humility, we can see the enemy for who he truly is – a cunning and deceitful adversary. Instead of relying on our own strength, we can lean on God's power and wisdom to face the challenges that come our way.

Moreover, humility opens our hearts to receive the depth of God's love. When we recognize our need for God's grace and forgiveness, we can experience the fullness of His love and mercy. God's love is unconditional, reaching far beyond our flaws and failures. It is in humility that we discover the beauty of God's redeeming love, transforming us from the inside out.

Here's To Hope: *Let us guard against the dangerous trap of pride. Instead, let us walk in humility, trusting in God's strength and wisdom. May we never underestimate the enemy, but also never underestimate the depth of God's love for us. In humility, we find hope, grace, and the assurance that we are not alone in this journey of life.*

DAY 37

Jesus Is Hope For Everyone Of Us Today.
Ephesians 1:18-21

I pray that the eyes of your heart may be enlightened in order that you may know the hope to which he has called you, the riches of his glorious inheritance in his holy people, and his incomparably great power for us who believe. That power is the same as the mighty strength he exerted when he raised Christ from the dead and seated him at his right hand in the heavenly realms, far above all rule and authority, power and dominion, and every name that is invoked, not only in the present age but also in the one to come.

Many of us know what it is to attach our hope to something or someone with expectations that this thing or that person could somehow deliver to us some measure of happiness.

But, there are a lot of us who have attached our hopelessness to something or someone as well.
Because our expectations were not met, we have become disappointed, jaded, and cynical about nearly anything that promises any measure of hope.

Yet, there is a Hope that never disappoints.

No matter what we have done.
No matter where we have been.
No matter how far away we may feel.
No matter what anyone else thinks.
No matter what anyone else may say.
No matter how many chances we have blown.
No matter how many times they have disappointed you.
No matter how many times you have disappointed you.

Jesus still pursues.
Jesus still forgives.

Jesus still loves.
Jesus still extends grace.
Jesus still restores.
Jesus still reconciles.
Jesus still redeems.
Jesus still heals.
Jesus still greets us with new mercies this morning.

We can anchor our hope in the one source that never disappoints – Jesus. Many of us have experienced the highs and lows of attaching our hope to various things or people, only to be let down and left feeling hopeless. But in Jesus, there is a hope that surpasses all our expectations.

No matter where we've been or what we've done, Jesus still pursues us with unwavering love. He is not deterred by our past mistakes or failures; instead, He offers forgiveness and restoration. Jesus doesn't just love us on our best days; He loves us consistently and unconditionally.

In a world full of broken promises and shattered dreams, Jesus remains faithful. He extends His grace to us freely, covering our shortcomings and offering us a fresh start each day. His love and mercy are not contingent on our performance; they are gifts given to us simply because He loves us.

When our hope is in Jesus, we can find peace even in the midst of life's uncertainties. He is our rock, our refuge, and our anchor. When we feel lost and overwhelmed, we can turn to Jesus, knowing that He will guide us through every storm.

Here's To Hope: *Let us place our hope in the One who never disappoints. Jesus is the source of unending hope, and His love has the power to transform our lives. No matter what we've been through or how far we may feel from Him, Jesus is still reaching out to us with open arms. There is hope for everyone, and that hope is found in Jesus. Let us embrace His love and grace and experience the true hope that only He can provide.*

DAY 38

Celebrate Jesus.

Philippians 1:6
And I am sure of this, that he who began a good work in you will bring it to completion at the day of Jesus Christ.

Today isn't the celebration of our own faithfulness to Jesus.
Today we're not celebrating our own worthiness.
Today we celebrate the faithfulness of Jesus to us.
Today we celebrate that only Jesus is worthy of worship.

And we celebrate that Jesus hasn't yet finished working in us and through us to become the faithful followers He has called us to be. We have every reason to celebrate Jesus today.

Today, we lift up the name of Jesus and celebrate His unwavering faithfulness to us. He is the One who began a good work in each of us, and He is the One who will bring it to completion.

As we come together in worship, we fix our eyes on Jesus, the author, and perfecter of our faith. He is the reason for our celebration, for He is the one who gave His life for us, demonstrating the depth of His love and grace. It is His faithfulness that sustains us, even in our moments of weakness and doubt.

Today, we lay down our burdens, knowing that Jesus is at work in us, transforming us day by day into His image. We may stumble and fall, but His grace is always there to lift us up and lead us forward. Our hope is not in our own abilities or merits, but in the faithfulness of our Savior, who never leaves us or forsakes us.

In the midst of life's challenges and uncertainties, we can be sure of one thing: Jesus is faithful. He is faithful to forgive, faithful to restore, and faithful to lead us on the path of righteousness. We celebrate His faithfulness today, knowing that He is always at work in us, guiding us toward the day of His glorious return.

Here's To Hope: *Let us lift our voices in praise and worship, giving thanks for the faithfulness of Jesus. He is the anchor of our hope, the source of our joy, and the reason for our celebration. May our lives be a reflection of His faithfulness, and may we continue to trust in Him with unwavering confidence. Today, and every day, we have every reason to celebrate Jesus.*

DAY 39

Jesus Makes Us Clean.

Hebrews 9:14

How much more, then, will the blood of Christ, who through the eternal Spirit offered himself unblemished to God, cleanse our consciences from acts that lead to death, so that we may serve the living God!

God's love for us today is not contingent upon:
Our progress reports,
Our track records,
Our wins,
Our losses,
Our successes,
Our failures,
Our history,
Our potential,
The number of times we have attended church,
The number of times we haven't,
The number of chances we have been given,
The number of times we have blown it,
How we compare to everyone else,
How much money we give,
How far away we may feel,
What anyone else thinks,
What anyone else says.

God's love for us is shown by sending Jesus to be the sacrifice to forgive every wrong word we have ever spoken, every wrong action we have ever committed, and every wrong thought we have ever pondered.

Jesus has taken away all of it.
Every bit of it.

We come before God today completely forgiven.
We are spotless.
We are clean.
We are made new.
All because of Jesus.
Only because of Jesus.

God's love for us is not conditional on our performance or achievements. It is not based on how well we have done or how many times we have failed. God's love is not swayed by our track records, successes, or losses. His love is not dependent on our history, or potential.

God's love for us is unchanging, unwavering, and unconditional. It is not affected by what others may think or say about us. His love is not earned by the amount of money we give or the good deeds we do. We don't have to strive to earn God's love because it is freely given to us.

The reason we can stand before God today, forgiven and free, is because of Jesus. He willingly became the sacrifice for our sins, taking upon Himself the weight of every wrong word, action, and thought we have ever had. He bore it all on the cross so that we could be made clean and new.

In Christ, we are forgiven. We are washed clean. We are made spotless. No sin is too great for His forgiveness, and no mistake is beyond His grace. Through Jesus, we have access to the boundless love of God, a love that covers all our shortcomings and failures.

Here's To Hope: *Let us rejoice in His love and grace. Let us remember that we are accepted and loved just as we are, not because of anything we have done, but because of everything Jesus has done for us. Our hope is secure in His unchanging love, and we can rest in the knowledge that we are fully and completely loved by our Heavenly Father. Only because of Jesus, we are forgiven and set free.*

DAY 40

God Is The Potter. We Are The Clay.

Isaiah 45:9
"Woe to him who strives with him who formed him, a pot among earthen pots! Does the clay say to him who forms it, 'What are you making?' or 'Your work has no handles'?

God is the Potter.
God is the Creator.
God is the Author.

We are the clay.
We are the creation.
Our stories are still being written.

When we forget this,
when we pretend to be more than we are,
it always leads to fear, worry, and anxiety.

God is God.
We are not.

Our lives are a canvas on which God is crafting a masterpiece. When we pretend to be more than we are and strive to be our own gods, it only leads to fear, worry, and anxiety. We were never meant to carry the weight of the world on our shoulders or to be in charge of our own destiny.

God, in His infinite wisdom and love, has designed each of us uniquely and intentionally. He knows the plans He has for us, plans for good and not for evil, plans to give us a future and a hope. He knows what is best for us, and He is capable of bringing beauty out of the messiest situations.

The verse from Isaiah reminds us not to strive with our Maker, not to question His work or doubt His plan. We can trust that God's hands are steady, and His work has a purpose and a design that we may not always understand. Instead of trying to control our own lives, let us surrender to the loving hands of the Potter, allowing Him to shape us into vessels of honor and vessels of His love.

As we embrace our position as clay in the hands of the Divine Potter, we find peace, security, and hope. We can rest in the knowledge that God is in control and that His plans for us are far greater than we can imagine.

Here's To Hope: *Let us trust in His craftsmanship, knowing that He is molding us into vessels that will bring glory to His name. Today, we surrender our lives to the Potter, allowing Him to continue His good work in us, and we find hope in the knowledge that He is the Author of our story, and it is a story of love, grace, and redemption.*

ABOUT THE AUTHOR

Sterling Edwards is a pastor and church planting catalyst. Together with his wife, Jenna, he shares a beautiful family of four daughters, one son-in-law, and two cherished grandsons. Sterling's life journey has been marked by a passion for ministry and a commitment to spreading the message of hope and faith in Jesus.

As an author, Sterling's insights and experiences come alive in his devotional writings, guiding readers on a journey of hope, faith, and the transformative power of God's love. Through his words, he invites readers to embrace a deeper relationship with God, finding solace, encouragement, and inspiration to navigate life's challenges with unwavering hope and unyielding faith.

Made in United States
Orlando, FL
10 July 2024